TALMAGE MCLAURIN, AIFD

FLOWER
styling

about the author

Talmage McLaurin, AIFD, is publisher at Florists' Review Enterprises, the floral industry's oldest and only independent publishing house, where he has worked for more than 20 years.

He began his career in his family's flower shop, learning the trade and beginning to hone his design style. Today, his designs regularly appear in *Florists' Review* magazine, along with his monthly column, "Trendspotting."

Talmage was honored in 2008 with the American Institute of Floral Designers' (AIFD) Award of Distinguished Service to the Floral Industry. He has been an AIFD member since 1988 and has shared his expertise with presentations at the National Symposium five times. In 2003, he co-chaired the National Symposium, The Prairie School.

His work has been featured in 15 books from Florists' Review Enterprises. This volume brings together some of Talmage's favorite designs, as well as new creations, which showcase his talent for styling botanicals in intriguing and new ways.

In memory of Dolores McLaurin (1943-2011) who first taught me to arrange flowers.

*The best inspirations
are found in nature.*

garden

8

*Bold and modern
takes on the traditional.*

graphic

38

*Celebrating the bounty
of the fall season.*

harvest

68

*Seasonal standouts
featuring the color red.*

holiday

98

garden

The best place to learn about flower arranging is in the garden. Following the patterns and nuances found in nature – as it celebrates freedom and embraces the happenstance – can breathe new life into even the simplest of compositions. In fact, when things aren't going quite right with a design, I stand back and ask myself, "Would it grow this way?"

PREVIOUS SPREAD Resplendent garden cuttings more often than not find their way from the potting shed into the living room, styled traditionally with the formality they deserve. Sorbet-colored garden roses, miniature callas (*Zantedeschias*) and hyacinths glow in this simple styling. TIP: Dimensional placements, created by varying the height of each flower, give each blossom a featured billing. *Photo by Mark Robbins*

LEFT Antique juice glasses positioned in wreath formation hold an enchanting collection of garden miniatures. Tiny *Anthuriums*, China asters (*Callistephus*), *Freesias*, spray roses, chrysanthemums, feverfew, deer foot ferns, Queen Anne's lace (*Ammi*) and small coral bells (*Heuchera*) leaves round out the delicate mix. TIP: To maximize the impact of miniature compositions, try elevating them on cake plates or plateaus. *Photo by Stephen Smith*

PREVIOUS SPREAD Simple mass compositions, while often considered basic, can transcend the common when expertly arranged. A carefully selected color story and layers of dimension are design elements that can elevate a simple gathering into an artful expression. Peonies, *Alliums*, roses, coral bells (*Heuchera*), lilacs, *Watsonia* and *Verbena* create a lush, garden homage. TIP: While the colors in this arrangement are predominantly pink, carefully chosen hints of purple and red invigorate the collection. *Photo by Mark Robbins*

LEFT The Victorians had a knack for presenting garden flowers – in fact, the home-grown variety was all that was available to them. That's probably why their containers are so befitting the garden style. The celebration basket, which later became associated solely with funerals, is still a nostalgic favorite of mine. The pastel hues of assorted roses, snowballs (*Viburnums*), *Alliums* and vining jasmine, along with branches of flowering quince and coral pea vine, enhance the basket's handle. TIP: Affordably priced baskets are readily available in antique stores. A light coat of spray paint spruces them up. *Photo by Mark Robbins*

Displaying specimen blossoms under glass can heighten their appeal. Here a prolific stem of *Cymbidium* orchids is accompanied by accents of fern fronds, ninebark (*Physocarpus*), *Scabiosa* and poppy pods, faux vine, and verdant, pearl-like strings of *Hypericum* berries. TIP: Remove *Hypericum* berries from their stems and thread them onto beading wire to create garland. *Photo by Stephen Smith*

This design, contained in a leaf-covered pot, promotes interest by inverting the *Galax* leaves and showcasing the individual direction of each stem. The mood is organic and irregular and cleverly relaxed, mirroring the way nature embraces the happenstance and celebrates the odd expression. TIP: Coat the backs of the *Galax* leaves with spray adhesive and press them onto the pot in an overlapping manner. *Photo by Stephen Smith*

RIGHT Twin containers merge their contents into a vivid "textile" of textured blossoms. The riotous screen of florals features royal blue *Hydrangeas* and *Delphiniums* contrasted with the complementary rusty orange cockscombs (*Celosia*), *Gloriosa* lilies and *Hypericums*. TIP: When designing multiple containers that will be displayed together, to conserve materials, create them as a unit rather than two arrangements that are later pushed together. *Photo by John Collins*

LEFT This modern interpretation of the garden topiary starts with a trunk of smooth stems that extends the pattern of the ribbed aluminum vase. At its peak, a dimensional cluster of lilies-of-the-valley (*Convallaria*), *Alliums*, snowballs (*Viburnums*), peonies, spray roses and mint leaves replaces traditional manicured foliages with a burst of fragrance and color. TIP: A floral-foam-filled cylinder hidden within the vertical stems holds the blossoms in place. *Photo by Mark Robbins*

I have never studied the Japanese art of flower arranging, yet I find it the most attractive of all disciplines to my personal aesthetic. Here, in an antique *Usubata*, I have given it a go. Although one might argue that *Ikebana* is not a garden style, its respect for nature and how things grow makes it the perfect garden match to me. Safflower stems stripped of foliage and blossoms are inverted in this traditional Asian urn featuring a single *Dahlia* bloom. Floating leaves at the base suggest the serenity of nature. TIP: A pin-frog flower holder, or *kenzan*, secures the initial placements as additional insertions are interwoven. *Photo by Stephen Smith*

A bold combination of only three elements – roses, *Hydrangeas* and *Hypericum* – forms a dimensionally rich, modern mixture of textures and colors while never losing its garden roots. TIP: Using multiple colors or varieties of the same flower instantly implies a garden aesthetic. *Photo by Stephen Smith*

The gentle roundness of this vintage wooden bowl underscores the curvature of the collection of succulents that it supports. Positioned on a wreath of floral foam, hidden just below the rim of the bowl, each cutting is secured with a small wooden pick. TIP: Once disassembled, the plants easily can be rooted.

RIGHT Autumn brings the garden a variety of color palettes, many of which stray far from the traditional warm tones. Here the cool blue-grays of the *Echeverias* and ornamental kale; the creamy white of the pumpkins; and the violet hues from the Michaelmas daisies (*Aster novi-belgii*), cottage yarrow (*Achillea*) and *Tracheliums* form a color harmony that approaches pastel. Clusters of brown millet (*Setaria*) and wheat add an iconic touch. TIP: Create a runner of polished river stones, lining up its edges with a yardstick. *Photos by Stephen Smith*

American garden style can run the gamut from complex to simple. Context often is the defining factor, as with these modern cuttings of *Zinnias* and *Coleus* and geranium leaves. TIP: Create a grid across the top of the glass vases with clear waterproof tape to hold the cuttings in place. *Photo by Stephen Smith*

RIGHT Like a cheery planted windowbox, this woven wall pocket corrals a wild grouping of colorful flowers and foliages. Sweeping lines capture the spirit of the botanicals in their natural state, as if plucked from the garden or country road. Wild and hybrid tea roses, peonies, *Verbena*, honeysuckle, *Leptospermum* and *Caladium* leaves compose the faux planting. TIP: Roadsides and untended gardens are great sources for interesting materials to mix with commercially grown blooms. *Photo by Mark Robbins*

LEFT A collection of elevated vases forms a modern hydroponic garden. Roses, miniature callas, *Phalaenopsis* orchids and mossy green *Dianthuses* cluster to form an organic statement. Whips of lily grass link the transparent vessels. TIP: Bring the garden style to events with the addition of inexpensive gems and jewels. Pearled wristlets decorate the vases and votives while premium picks mingle among the flowers. *Photo by John Collins*

This casual collection of gardeny materials features bells-of-Ireland, spray chrysanthemums, *Hydrangeas*, loosestrife (*Lysimachia*), Canterbury bells (*Campanula*), rice flower and fresh wheat. TIP: Organically shaped vases with irregular lines are fitting receptacles for modern garden collections. *Photo by Stephen Smith*

Magically capturing nature under glass, this garden cloche features the cool colorings of *Hydrangeas*, cockscombs (*Celosia*), figs and dill while showcasing a pine-straw nest filled with natural quail eggs. TIP: A small tray of floral foam attaches to the glass base with florists' clay and invisibly holds the materials in place.

RIGHT New varieties of classic garden staples – 'Super Green' roses and varieties of blue and green *Hydrangeas* – are sectioned into groups to highlight their unique textures. Clusters of lily grass (*Liriope*) form sweeping, dynamic lines that give the urns a modern edge. TIP: Insert lily grass so that it lines the insides of the vases, creating an interesting network of stems and grasses. *Photos by Stephen Smith*

Sporting a wire mesh midsection, this metal urn affords the perfect mechanic for a texture-rich weaving of prairie grasses. In elegant contrast to the earthy base, a pairing of 'Chippendale' and 'Piano' garden-style roses elegantly finishes the composition. TIP: Lacking a hydration source, the grasses and grains will shrink over time. To compensate for this, allow the grass-woven urn to sit overnight and fill in any gaps before arranging the flowers. *Photo by Stephen Smith*

RIGHT My love affair with garden-style roses is celebrated in this arrangement of seven varieties. 'Darcey', 'Patience', 'Mariatheresia', 'Piano', 'Baronesse', 'Aphrodite' and 'Augusta Luise' fill these vases with incomparable splendor. TIP: Displaying collections of vases is en vogue. Be on the lookout for inexpensive flea market and antique store finds. *Photo by John Collins*

The fan-shaped finger vase, also referred to as Quintal horns, was designed especially for supporting heavy, short-stemmed flowers. The oldest examples show up in the Netherlands in the 18th century, but the containers were also the rage in England, from which they came to Colonial America. Filled with garden cuttings, these vases were quite possibly the first flower-specific container in America. An updated version from the Williamsburg Pottery factory holds a traditional fan of millet (*Setaria*), montbretia (*Crocosmia*) pods, *Brunia* and *Thryptomene*. TIP: Experiment with combinations of dried and fresh materials, displaying an interesting contrast of textures. *Photo by Stephen Smith*

RIGHT This blended mass of vertically positioned botanicals is both gardeny and modern in its styling. The materials, including garden *Irises*, *Alliums*, foxtail lilies (*Eremurus*), larkspurs (*Delphinium*), lily grass (*Liriope*) and coral bells (*Heuchera*) leaves, occupy only a small plot and tower upward in a visual "dance" of color and texture that mimics abstract expression. TIP: Weave lily grass through the mass of flowers, giving unity to the collection of dissimilar materials. *Photo by Mark Robbins*

LEFT I'm in love with aged wooden surfaces. From antique furniture to simple kitchen utensils, the pattern and texture of the grain always win me over. My oversized wooden dough bowl is filled with luxury beyond its humble intentions with this extravagant collection of garden roses, fringed tulips, *Hydrangeas*, hyacinths and waxflowers. TIP: Line wooden containers with waterproof floral polyfoil to protect them.

Designing en masse, which composes the bulk of arrangements made in the Western world, can enlist a variety of approaches. For this pink-glazed pot of springtime merriment, clusters of tulips, hyacinths, peonies and *Ranunculi* are placed casually in groupings that showcase each variety and flower. TIP: Bind the clusters of soft-stemmed flowers with waterproof tape near the base of the stems to provide stability before placement into floral foam.
Photos by Stephen Smith

The oxblood pigment of this vintage Chinese rice basket accentuates the red markings found in the *Cymbidium* orchid throats, *Anthurium* spadices, pomegranate skins and rose hips while the lavender hues of the chrysanthemums and verdant greens of the *Cymbidiums* and *Anthuriums* enliven the color mix. TIP: Groupings emphasize each flower type while maintaining the distinctive ease found in American garden style.

RIGHT An abundance of premium flowers fills this wrought-iron garden vase stuffed with *Hydrangea* blossoms. A velvety carpet of burgundy cockscombs (*Celosia*) surrounds the base and is repeated as trim. Oriental lilies, snowballs (*Viburnums*), *Dahlias*, pincushions (*Leucospermums*), staghorn ferns, lady's mantle (*Alchemilla*), and hanging *Amaranthus* outfit this arrangement with style. The distinctive golden marigold garland, ubiquitous in Nepalese and Indian cultures, confirms the urn's South Asian flair. TIP: The *Hydrangeas* maintain their freshness with the help of large water picks hidden within the urn. *Photos by Stephen Smith*

graphic

Gaining attention in a visually overwhelmed world – where subtlety and understatement often go unnoticed – is no small challenge, even for flower designers. That's why bold, graphic statements are finding their way back in fashion. High-impact colors and geometry lead the charge in a look that is as refined and artful as it is bold and assertive.

PREVIOUS SPREAD Contained in a row of contemporary nickel vases inspired by classic Chinese shapes, choice faux *Ranunculi* swirl and spin into an abstract portrait that mimics modern expressionist art. TIP: Choose heavily weighted vases or fill them with sand or gravel to stabilize the dramatically sweeping stems.

RIGHT Showcasing cut orchids in flower designs calls for innovative methods of presenting just a few stems. Here orbs of randomly woven blades of variegated lily grass (*Liriope*) deftly display two stems of *Phalaenopsis* orchids to their best advantage. The accent of "organic" ribbon was fabricated by pressing strips of variegated *Aspidistra* leaves between two pieces of clear packing tape.
TIP: Form the orbs by weaving individual blades of grass into a wire ornament or into chicken wire that has been shaped into a sphere. *Photos by Stephen Smith*

LEFT A cluster of fan-shaped *Fatsia* leaves positioned in a well-ordered formation offers a declaration to the power of simple, deliberate expression. 'Moonaqua' carnations carpet the surface of two of the three cubes in a splash of commanding color. TIP: Aquarium gravel provides an affordable and attractive surface treatment for topping off designs with minimal placements. *Photo by John Collins*

Small glass vases are perfect for displaying broken and short-stemmed flowers. This modern take on an old-fashioned bubble bowl comprises a potpourri of fresh orchid blossoms and grass clippings. TIP: Fill the bowl with short pieces of bear grass in a crisscross manner that provides an armature to elevate the blooms. *Photo by Stephen Smith*

I am fascinated by the way water magically distorts submerged materials. That's why I am often more interested in what is happening below the water line than above it. In neoclassical splendor, this modernized urn reveals clustered *Cymbidium* orchids interrupted by lily grass (*Liriope*) bundles neatly wrapped with decorative silver wire. TIP: Position each orchid into the vase so that the throats and petals are visible and the stems are out of sight.

RIGHT Updating classic shapes with floral enhancements can be transformational. Eye-catching stripes are featured at the exaggerated base of this traditional urn overflowing with *Phalaenopsis* orchids. 'Green Trick' *Dianthuses*, carnations and spray mums have been pavéd in alternating rows onto a jumbo block of floral foam. A delicate string of *Hypericum* berries adds a graceful note. TIP: String individual berries onto beading wire to create the *Hypericum* garland. *Photos by Stephen Smith*

To celebrate flowers in the extreme, try an arrangement that is all flowers, including the container. An extravagant collection of orchids finds a lush home nestled into a block of tightly packed carnations. TIP: Create the flower-covered "vase" by placing a brick of floral foam upright on a tray and covering the sides of the foam with rows of carnations.

RIGHT Cheeriness is communicated in many ways, but who can argue with the youthful optimism of brightly colored stripes? Here, paired with a colorful burst of *Dahlias* and miniature *Gerberas*, an elevated vase is resurfaced with horizontal rows of overlapping electrical tape in a rainbow of colors, creating a design that exudes happiness. TIP: Mold a framework of chicken wire into the interior of containers with large openings to provide an armature to hold stems in place. *Photos by Stephen Smith*

LEFT Nothing in nature approaches abstract expression quite like clouds. As with flowers, their ephemeral beauty has captured the attention of artists from painters to poets. These cloudlike vases are filled with fluffy baby's breath (*Gypsophila*), stocks and *Dahlias* in a peaceful mass. *Anthuriums* and *Gerberas* add contrast of texture and color. TIP: Fill the vases first with the baby's breath, and use its structure to position the remaining insertions. *Photo by Bill Boyd*

Natural sculpture, like this gnarled grapewood, provides both a striking graphic and a useful positioning tool for six exquisite stems of amaryllises (*Hippeastrum*). TIP: Secure the trio of vases to the tray with waterproof adhesive for easy transport. *Photo by John Collins*

Blurring the lines between display and design, this collection of glass vases gives each botanical its due. Fern fronds, roses, *Cymbidium* orchids, *Hosta* leaves and *Hydrangeas* each are featured in their individual glass containment. TIP: When sourcing containers, choose differing shapes to keep the grouping eclectic.

RIGHT Almost any smooth-sided urn can be transformed instantly with a surfacing of fresh tree leaves and lamb's ear (*Stachys*). Each selected for its durability and contrast of color, the leaves deliver a fashionable camouflage finish. TIP: A coating of spray adhesive and random positioning generate the simple-to-create yet handsome results. *Photos by Stephen Smith*

Leaf-covered vases have become almost commonplace among progressive flower arrangers, but inverting the leaves can add an unexpected twist. Variegated *Aspidistra* leaves and raspberry-colored callas (*Zantedeschias*) form this genius concept that I borrowed from a presentation by German design sensation Klaus Wagener.
TIP: A coat of spray adhesive efficiently attaches the leaves to a simple glass cylinder.

RIGHT Forming the universal shape that expresses love, these hearts are at once literal and modern in their message. 'Purple Mikado' and 'Macarena' spray roses lend their garden appeal in miniature alignment.
TIP: Arrange the short-stemmed roses in plastic-backed floral-foam hearts available at floral wholesalers and craft outlets. *Photos by Stephen Smith*

LEFT Manicured to near perfection, the normally free-spirited tulip is compacted between thin blades of steel grass, creating a trumpet-shaped form that modernizes the classic mint julep cup. TIP: To even their varied heights, gather the mixture of tulips and grass blades and gently invert them on a flat surface. Trim the ends, and place the mix into the julep cup. *Photo by Mark Robbins*

A wonderful trick of the eye occurs as this single 'Kissproof' lily appears to have grown through an unusually tall stack of salal leaves. The layered leaves exhibit textural interest that is made even more enchanting with the glass encasement. TIP: Gather salal leaves to fill the height of the container and use a hole punch to pierce each leaf so it can be threaded easily onto the lily stem. *Photo by Stephen Smith*

Flower presentations that show some unexpected wit are among my personal favorites. Here the common apple presents a graphic twist. To accommodate the single stem of lilies, the two stacked apples are cored. For the companion vase, the stacking reaches heights that are sure to collapse. Luckily it's just an illusion relying on a hyacinth stake's central piercing to keep things from tumbling down. TIP: Treat cored apples with a splash of lemon juice to inhibit discoloration.

RIGHT Even subtle colors can achieve graphic impact. In contrast to traditional designs, where stems radiate and never cross paths, a graphic statement is made with the intersecting stems of these French tulips. TIP: Position lanky tulip stems inside a deep cylinder to control their pendulous nature. Coordinating seashells further position the stems. *Photos by Stephen Smith*

LEFT Instant arrangements like this submerged stem of *Cymbidium* orchids require nothing more than the appropriate vase and properly prepared flower food solution to keep the water clean and clear. TIP: When arranging under water, choose foliage-free flowers with a waxy surface that won't waterlog. *Photo by John Collins*

The term "graphic" doesn't always imply in-your-face shock value or drama. Simple, innovative treatments – like filling the perimeter of a vase with 'Green Goddess' calla (*Zantedeschia*) blooms and featuring tulips in the center – make modern expressions that are captivating and novel. TIP: Choose a vase with rounded edges so that the callas will form to the interior of the container. *Photo by Stephen Smith*

PREVIOUS SPREAD These stone-shaped vases, with their organic curves, initiate a high-impact color contrast to the luxe choice of fuchsia *Phalaenopsis* orchids. This graphic statement is fluid, sensual and empowered by its bold color pairing. TIP: Choose containers and blossoms that are complementary in shape when creating a unified sculptural design. *Photo by John Collins*

Graphic tribal expression mixes beautifully with a modern aesthetic. This studied design mimics a hand-loomed weaving. Crossing stems of *Iris* foliage form the weave while contrasting roses, *Gerberas*, *Delphiniums*, cone flowers (*Echinacea*), *Lycopodium* and dill add texture and color.
TIP: Start with the vertical insertions of *Iris* foliage and flowers. Add the horizontal foliage after the other materials are in place. *Photo by Stephen Smith*

RIGHT Collections of found objects create a scrapbook of materials that hold emotional or spiritual meaning to the collector. With the look of an expertly arranged potpourri, this tray of materials includes botanical, natural and man-made materials. TIP: Bracing stems across the tray will add a woven feeling to the composition while holding other elements in place. *Photo by Stephen Smith*

While many graphic designs gravitate toward a sleek, modern incarnation, there are other ways to approach this style. This rustic design contrasts the textures of billy buttons (*Craspedia*) and *Anthuriums* against rough-hewn surfaces, like wood and concrete, to create a powerful statement with a completely different point of view. TIP: Use a floral-foam sphere as the base for the irregular mass of billy buttons. *Photo by Bill Boyd*

RIGHT The unexpected pairing of orchids, tangerines and clear glass makes a powerful graphic statement as the fruits and flowers float seemingly unsupported in a pair of sculptural vases. TIP: Fresh materials that are submerged should be chosen as much for their durability as their visual appeal. *Photo by John Collins*

LEFT Provocative color combinations advance fashion. Whether bold and clashing or subtle and harmonious, the shift of trendy colors keeps what's considered fashionable in constant flux. Here the current push for quirky palettes finds a modern spirit in the color combination alone. Warm hues of burgundy, lavender and purple in the Canterbury bells (*Campanula*), chocolate *Cosmos*, safflowers, lace flowers (*Trachymene*) and *Hypericum* are interrupted by the sharp lime-yellow complements of the *Cymbidium* orchids. TIP: Even mass arrangements can benefit from featured flowers to direct the eye and create contrasting focal areas.

This shadowbox of hyacinths is arranged in a manner that accommodates their free-spirited shifts as they continue to grow past their harvest. Surfacing from a dense field of bear grass, the blooms are encased by a canopy of lily grass (*Liriope*) stems that have been gently bent and woven over the top of the structure. TIP: Bear grass that is sheared evenly a few inches above the lip of the container gently positions the hyacinths in a natural, as-they-grow manner.
Photos by Stephen Smith

harvest

As far as seasons go, autumn is hands-down my favorite. The intoxicating smell of wood-burning fires, the textures of bundled grains and grasses, and the colors of turning leaves and ripe pumpkins all resonate with my soul. My favorite day of the year is the crisp morning when I first can sense that fall is in the air. For me, it's an automatic rush.

PREVIOUS SPREAD: An arrangement of found objects, like this one in my antique dough bowl, is often more exciting to me than the expected vase or basket of flowers. The elements, ever open to new configurations, include dried pomegranates, clove-studded orange pomanders, black walnuts, twig balls and wreaths formed from wild vines pulled from my flower beds. The roses are arranged in floral-foam orbs. TIP: Keep the wild rose vines fresh in water picks tucked into the composition. *Photo by Mark Robbins*

LEFT Providing perfect understatement for the parlor, this basket contains three of my favorite blossoms: garden roses, callas (*Zantedeschias*) and *Freesias*. Russet-colored coral bells (*Heuchera*) foliage supplies a distinctive accent instead of the expected greens. TIP: Garden foliages give even the most commercial blossoms a fresh-picked edge. *Photo by Stephen Smith*

What were once simple bowls of potpourri have evolved into chunky collections of artfully placed treasures that replace the expected vase of flowers or centerpiece. Centered with a pine-straw bird's nest, this seasonal grouping includes gourds, pine cones, oak leaves, acorns, Indian corn, wheat and grasses converging to capture the essence of the harvest. TIP: To add extra ambience to the collection, add a drop of autumnal-scented potpourri oil. *Photo by Stephen Smith*

RIGHT Affordable glass vases, based on the classic Chinese Ming vase, become magical when filled with a colorful potpourri of gourds, persimmons, hazelnuts and sweet-gum fruit. Such presentations revolutionize the notion that floral design is only about flowers or what emerges from a vase. TIP: To achieve a balance between materials, mix all the elements into a large box and pour them into the vase. *Photo by Mark Robbins*

LEFT A pavé of cushion chrysanthemums, yarrow (*Achillea*) and Queen Anne's lace (*Ammi*) resembles the gently rolling hills of an autumnal landscape. Square trays are covered with *Galax* leaves for an attractive organic border while clippings of lily grass (*Liriope*) add interesting visual interruptions when interspersed between the flowers. TIP: Coat the backs of the *Galax* leaves with floral adhesive and press onto the plastic trays, overlapping the leaves.

Tropical croton (*Codiaeum*) leaves are affixed with floral adhesive to an inexpensive container to make a pattern-rich vase. When filled with a gardenlike mix of safflowers (*Carthamus*), butterfly weed (*Asclepias*), black-eyed Susans (*Rudbeckia*) and kangaroo paws (*Anigozanthos*), the end-of-summer collection reprises the colors and patterns of the croton leaves with a dynamic burst of energy. TIP: Croton leaves are readily and affordably available in plant form. *Photos by Stephen Smith*

As a proponent of loosely styled arrangements, I always approach these designs with great caution. With increased freedom for expression, the basic principles and elements of design don't go away. Instead, they become increasingly important. This trio of vases, though arranged with great freedom, requires substantial focal flowers to justify the sweeping lines and deconstructed clusters. Without the buoyant *Dahlia* and the graphic green lotus pod, all would be lost. TIP: The addition of a few stems of lily grass (*Liriope*) affordably expands the size and presence of a design. *Photo by Stephen Smith*

RIGHT These Native American-inspired baskets are personal favorites from my brief dabbling in product development, though these samples never made it into production. The reproductions are based on a photograph of a museum exhibit that appealed to me, particularly because of my Cherokee heritage. The arrangement they hold has a tropical feel, with its miniature callas (*Zantedeschias*), *Hosta* and *Euonymus* foliage, and citron fruit. The pair of conch shells reinforces the emphasis on dual imagery. TIP: For a better economy of materials, place the conch shells into the design first and arrange the flowers around them. *Photo by Mark Robbins*

PREVIOUS SPREAD One of my favorite tricks (when designing multiple arrangements) is to place a large central element, such as these pumpkins, and design around it. The sizable central focal points create instant uniformity, allowing for more freedom when finishing the edges with a mixture of *Dahlias*, spray roses, pincushions (*Leucospermums*), *Ruscus*, montbretia (*Crocosmia*) pods and navy-colored ivy (*Hedera*) berries. TIP: Set the baskets on clear plates to protect linens and wood finishes.

LEFT From turkey feathers to the botanical inclusions of miniature callas (*Zantedeschias*), montbretia (*Crocosmia*) pods, billy buttons (*Craspedia*), kangaroo paws (*Anigozanthos*) and coneflowers (*Rudbeckia*), each element contributes to the abstract patterns formed from the crowding of parallel placements. TIP: Begin by creating a dimensional framework of birch branches, placing them vertically into the floral foam to brace the flower insertions.

Contained designs are those that are restricted by the form of the vessel in which they are displayed. Many fall into the category of "bouquets under glass," as does this example of callas (*Zantedeschias*) curling around the base of a modern glass vase. TIP: Choose flowers that are smooth and foliage-free to help keep the water clear. *Photos by Stephen Smith*

LEFT Flowers have the ability to express emotions when words can't be found. Their ephemeral nature reflects the fragility of the human condition, and this symbolism is never more eloquent than when marking life's passing. This traditional wreath, staged here in an autumnal setting, beautifully combines 'Sunny Leonidas', 'Pretty Woman', 'Sari', 'Orange Flame' and 'Tropical Amazone' roses. TIP: Today's foam-filled wreath forms make this formerly labor-intensive design process fast and easy and provide ample water reserve for the flowers. *Photo by Mark Robbins*

Many years ago, I discovered a Japanese design book that pictured elaborate displays of callas (*Zantedeschias*) entwined into knotted formations. The visual was so distinctive that I couldn't get it out of my head until I had tried my hand at the concept. Here are the results of my interpretation. This Italian terra-cotta urn was a perfect pairing with the warm tones of the 'Mango' miniature callas (*Zantedeschias*) and the velvety textures of the *Magnolia* leaves and twigs. TIP: Allow the callas to dehydrate for several hours before manipulation. Once in place, rehydrate the flowers to harden them to their original state. *Photo by Stephen Smith*

This pair of towering arrangements exudes the spirit of primitive craftsmanship with its vibrant color choices and its nod to mosaic color blocking with the pavé-style collection of blossoms at the base. Warm colors of montbretia (*Crocosmia*), cockscomb (*Celosia*), yarrow (*Achillea*), festival bush (*Ceratopetalum*), billy buttons (*Craspedia*), pincushions (*Leucospermums*) and oat grass (*Avena*) compose the vegetative design. TIP: It's best to hot-glue the tall container to the base container before adding flowers so the designs can be moved without disturbance. *Photo by Bill Boyd*

RIGHT Arrangements of such visual heavyweights as *Dahlias*, artichokes and pincushions (*Leucospermums*) benefit from the addition of lightweight materials like these *Gloriosa* lilies and date fruits, particularly when they form a floating layer above the compacted materials. At the base of the design, maple leaves showing their autumnal colors of deep oxblood, olive drab and burgundy provide an organic resurfacing. TIP: Transform a basic plastic bowl by covering the backs of the leaves with spray adhesive and pressing them onto the bowl. *Photo by Stephen Smith*

LEFT Foxtail millet (*Setaria*) gives these modern sheaves their cascading quality. The lush bursts are smartly topped with a focal point of 'Sari' roses, sunflower centers and *Alliums* arranged in a straight-handled bouquet holder that is slipped into the center of the millet sheaf. Tapered glass vases provide a perfect view of the stems to suggest the classic sheaf stalk. TIP: Grains and grasses fade quickly, so be sure to add a flower-food solution to keep the water clean.

The harvest sheaf of grain – iconic to the season – becomes a handsome container covering, here finished with a wrapping of utilitarian twine. Overflowing with harvest gatherings, the custom basket displays weighty artichokes and crests of cockscomb (*Celosia*) alongside clusters of billy buttons (*Craspedia*), *Scabiosa* pods, sneezeweed (*Helenium*), cone flowers (*Echinacea*) and China millet (*Setaria*). TIP: Use hot glue to position the grain on the papier-mâché container. *Photos by Stephen Smith*

These organically shaped vases come by their description naturally. Dried gourds are repurposed by cutting off the tops and slipping water tubes inside. Then the balance-challenged gourds are secured into place with bits of old-fashioned florists' clay to display two varieties of spray chrysanthemums. TIP: Because water tubes only hold a small amount of water, choose flowers that are not heavy drinkers, like these chrysanthemums. *Photos by Stephen Smith*

RIGHT Nothing transforms a table as quickly and effectively as a runner. The turning leaves of the sweet-gum tree form a path of color and texture. Assorted baskets punctuate the leafy surface with varied collections featuring 'Leonidas' roses, pumpkin-colored spider mums and Asian pears. Clippings of steel grass, fresh dill and montbretia (*Crocosmia*) pods add texture and dynamic lines to the low-lying gatherings. TIP: Spray the leaves with adhesive and press onto a sheet of thick kraft paper.

The three fused cylinders of this glass vase provide the perfect, unobtrusive containment for a field of autumn grasses and fall-hued blossoms. Pumpkin-colored *Gerberas*, *Amaranthus*, cone flowers (*Echinacea*) and Chinese lantern lilies (*Sandersonias*) combine with black-beard wheat and bear grass for a nature study that celebrates the playful interplay between the high-contrast materials. TIP: In fall designs, consider adding dried materials to the mix for their seasonal contrast of texture and color.
Photo by Stephen Smith

RIGHT Most flowers purchased in the United States are gifted, bearing with them feelings of thanks, sympathy, congratulations or love. This pocket-basket of *Freesias*, *Ranunculi* and orchids could express any of those sentiments when left to be discovered on the garden gate. TIP: When baskets need water-proofing, I line them with plastic-coated foil made for wrapping potted plants.
Photo by Mark Robbins

Once considered the result of poorly executed design, the crossed lines in this composition are purposely placed to create its essential tension. The disparate materials, including yarrow (*Achillea*), coneflowers (*Rudbeckia*), kangaroo paws (*Anigozanthos*) and *Hypericum*, form a botanical tapestry infused with rhythm and movement. **TIP:** Secure the candles into the floral foam by drilling three holes into the bottom of each candle and inserting wooden picks vertically. *Photo by Stephen Smith*

The simple water tube has long been the answer to saving a stem that is too short to make it to a water source, but this might be taking the technique to the extreme. A vine-wrapped tomato cage, its stakes clipped away, provides the framework supporting two rings of multiple clear water tubes towering over an antique pewter tureen. *Dahlias, Ranunculi, Gloriosas, Alliums* and *Gaillardias* decorate the structure. TIP: For an affordable alternative to glass, choose plastic water tubes, and secure them with paper-covered wire.

RIGHT One modern approach to outfitting a dining table – commonly referred to as tablescaping – deconstructs the traditional centerpiece into a menagerie of coordinated components. Central to this autumnal collection is a floral-foam orb tightly packed with texture-rich roses, chrysanthemums, safflowers (*Carthamus*), *Hypericum* berries and the velvety centers of petal-plucked *Gerberas*. Glowing pillar candles, held snugly in place with tufts of berries, seeded *Eucalyptus* and nuts, revolve around the central sphere of blended botanicals. A scattering of gourds, nuts and *Magnolia* foliage completes the fall tableau. TIP: Add a sense of spontaneity to a manicured form with a spiral of decorative wire on the outer surface. *Photos by Stephen Smith*

LEFT An amber collection of seashells and natural sponges decorates this glass cube from the inside out, providing a captivating container for an unconventional mixture of garden and exotic blossoms. Pincushions (*Leucospermums*), roses, *Hydrangeas*, butterfly weed (*Asclepias*), cone flowers (*Echinacea*), cockscomb (*Celosia*) and *Berzelia* combine for a high-end mixture. TIP: Elevate the drama of most any arrangement by placing it onto a tray or pedestal.

The notion that a well-crafted flower design has to be complicated or difficult to make is a myth to me. The designs that delight me the most are those that show calculated restraint, allowing the beauty of the blossoms to be unobscured by manipulation and adornment. TIP: Here, rare orchids are styled simply and are exquisitely presented by simple elevation and gentle clustering to show off their matchless perfection. *Photos by Stephen Smith*

holiday

Red is synonymous with the celebration of Christmas. Two months later, it appears again as the signature color of Valentine's Day. Retail florists wouldn't survive without this passionate primary in their palette. That's why it's only appropriate that the most powerful of all colors is featured in designs that represent my holiday point of view.

PREVIOUS SPREAD This unadorned vase of 'Black Magic' roses is flanked by two collections – one contained in an antique dough bowl and the other displayed under a glass cloche. The assortments of natural found objects and handblown glass create the impression of a lovingly collected vignette while remaining effortless in the presentation. TIP: The addition of a few ornaments gives a seasonless display an instant holiday transformation.

RIGHT The carnation retains all the qualities that originally made it one of the most popular commercial blossoms. Its wide range of colors, long vase life, year-round availability and clovelike fragrance make it prime for an overdue comeback. With their fluffy texture and affordability, the blooms are perfect in mass presentations such as this classic holiday wreath. TIP: Dip each stem in floral adhesive before insertion into the floral-foam wreath to increase durability. *Photos by Stephen Smith*

LEFT I like to call this combination of colors "super-red." It's a phenomenon born of the popularity of analogous harmonies (hues next to each other on the color wheel), and here it is achieved by combining orange-reds, pink-reds, burgundy-reds and true reds for heightened impact. Roses, *Ranunculi*, *Gloriosas*, *Gerberas*, carnations and rose hips tell this sophisticated story. TIP: Hold back smaller buds and the delicate *Gloriosas*, and make them the final, slightly elevated insertions to the design.

Clear glass can present a positioning challenge when there is more vase than available stems. This lovely solution uses a mix of red and green dogwood (*Cornus*) stems to form a framework that is at once attractive to look at and useful to the arranger. Stars-of-Bethlehem (*Ornithogalums*), *Viburnum* berries, *Lysimachia*, snowberries, mint and scented geranium leaves complete the gardeny assemblage. TIP: Remove any foliage from the dogwood stems to avoid compromising the clearness of the water. *Photos by Stephen Smith*

Captivating and carnivorous stems of the cobra lily (*Sarracenia*) casually cross within this simple vase, featuring a single floating *Dahlia* blossom. The result is a design that is complex in its concept yet effortless in execution. TIP: To avoid waterlogging the *Dahlia* bloom, leave a little length on the stem to hold it slightly above the water.

RIGHT Fall *Dahlias*, available well into the holiday season, present perfect hues for wine tastings and other festive fêtes. Contrasting hues from deep burgundy to fuchsia form a captivating celebratory centerpiece. TIP: Insert the *Dahlias* into a floral-foam wreath form for easy construction.
Photos by Stephen Smith

LEFT Forming an exotic take on holiday flowers, what appears to be a long centerpiece is actually three containers brimming with unconventional materials. *Anthurium* blossoms and foliage, *Aechmea* bromeliad blooms, and pomegranates combine with the familiar sparks of spray roses and *Hypericum* for a transseasonal centerpiece. TIP: Insert wooden picks into the pomegranates to secure the fruits into the floral foam.

Since all my Jewish friends say the best place for dinner on Christmas Day is a Chinese restaurant, this clever collection might have an audience. An affordable transparent take-out box unites the holiday's iconic complementary colors with a cross-cultural twist. A verdant *Cymbidium* orchid floats above a red *Gerbera*, taking center stage among callas (*Zantedeschias*), chinaberries and two chopstick-resembling stems. TIP: A collection of these down the center of a table makes a witty and wonderful extended centerpiece.
Photos by Stephen Smith

Exquisite *Gloriosa* lilies are more affordable when purchased with shorter stem lengths. Presented here in monobotanical glory, the blossoms' visual value is maximized by this trio vase and candlestick combination. TIP: When arranging delicate flowers around candles, be aware that the heat will affect the blossoms' longevity. *Photo by Stephen Smith*

RIGHT While the amaryllis (*Hippeastrum*) is at its finest when displayed with a full length of stem, the blossoms are also exceptional when clustered into a mound of magical blooms. Here, finding a featured spot next to the tree, this white variety with red markings makes the holidays bright. TIP: To sturdy the awkward stems, wrap the bundle of amaryllis with waterproof tape in nosegay style. *Photo by John Collins*

LEFT Arranging flowers in a V formation may be one of my favorite things to do. While respecting the rules of relative symmetry and a central binding point – both hallmarks of traditional Western design – it turns the expected triangle upside down, evoking a freedom that I can only describe as "taking flight." Miniature *Cymbidium* orchids, miniature callas (*Zantedeschias*), *Dahlias* and *Hydrangeas* compose this striking departure from the norm. TIP: Styling is important to dramatic designs. The small bowl of unshelled pecans, positioned beneath the canopy of callas, extends the impact of the display. *Photo by Mark Robbins*

Rich, velvety textures of scented geranium foliage accentuate the deep burgundy *Dahlias*, *Leucadendrons*, carnations, *Hypericum*, *Cosmos* and *Lophomyrtus* and the detailed markings of the *Paphiopedilum* orchids. Compacted yet loosely combined, this cluster embodies the essence of contemporary garden style. TIP: For short-stemmed orchids, use water-filled picks to provide an appropriate reservoir for the blossoms. *Photo by Stephen Smith*

Candlesticks are smart props for these restrained centerpieces of 'Red Delicious' abundance. A no-frills crystal bowl filled with these seasonal favorites ties together the satellite combinations of cockscomb (*Celosia*) and apples. TIP: Atop the candlesticks, each fruit is carefully balanced and secured into the floral foam with multiple wooden picks. *Photo by John Collins*

RIGHT Red roses, cockscomb (*Celosia*) and *Hypericum* berries form an interpretive topiary elevated on a silver trumpet-styled vase. The composition is softened by a fringe of shiny *Camellia* leaves and fragrant cedar. TIP: Build the design in a straight-handled bouquet holder and slip it into the vase. *Photo by Mark Robbins*

Science fuses with nature in this unexpected presentation of classic red roses, which nestle in extenders originally designed to hold candles for centerpiece designs. The replacement of stems with bubble-bearing glass rods creates a fascinating surprise. TIP: Create depth by varying the lengths of the glass extenders. Here they are cut to differing heights.

RIGHT The pairing of fruit with flowers and foliages is an American holiday tradition going back to colonial days. At that time, evergreens and fruits were choices of necessity. This modern-day combination is chosen for both aesthetic and nostalgic reasons; turns out, the colonial limitations produced lovely results. Here, apples, limes and pomegranates join roses, cockscomb (*Celosia*), snowberries and variegated *Pittosporum* in a modern take on the colonial tradition. TIP: To avoid debris clouding the water, arrange flowers in another smaller container tucked inside the collection of fruits.
Photos by Stephen Smith

A single red rose and a heart shape could mean only one thing. Valentine's Day, the king of flower holidays, strains the supply of red roses like no other event. This single specimen – appropriately named 'Cherry Love' – finds a home among the evenly trimmed stems of *Equisetum* packed snugly to take on the heart shape of the vase when viewed from above. TIP: Remove all foliage and thorns from the rose stem so that it slips easily into the *Equisetum* bundle.
Photo by Stephen Smith

RIGHT Carnations, when presented en masse, take on an elegant air that defies their often-maligned reputation. Floral-foam wreaths at each level make the lush configuration easy and fast to execute. TIP: For added depth, when arranging a mass of a single flower, choose two varieties in slightly differing colors.
Photo by Mark Robbins

LEFT Being Scottish, I've always had an affinity for tartan plaids. Mixing and matching the patterns promotes a modern aesthetic. TIP: The illusion of a rose sphere is created by shaving a rectangular piece of floral foam into a round formation and arranging the roses on that surface.

If flower foam revolutionized the floral industry, foam spheres revolutionized the world of flower foam. With unprecedented popularity among flower design fashionistas, these orbs have been covered with most every plant material imaginable. Here, with a touch of nostalgia, the unassuming carnation shares the geometry with vibrantly reflective miniature glass ornaments and pearl-headed corsage pins. TIP: Dip the flower stems in waterproof floral adhesive before arranging so the stems will remain in place as they shrink over time. Keep the stems short; deep insertions into the foam sphere weaken the structure. *Photos by Stephen Smith*

Peeking out the top of this lustrous vase of glazed earthenware, *Dahlias*, *Hydrangeas*, *Hypericum* berries, coral bells (*Heuchera*) foliage and curly fern fronds illustrate the style of reverse proportion. In these designs, the container rather than the botanicals occupies the majority of the composition. TIP: Instead of filling the entire vase with floral foam, fill the bottom with packing materials and insert a small plastic liner at the top. *Photo by Stephen Smith*

RIGHT One amaryllis (*Hippeastrum*) is a fantastic thing to see, but a vase full of the gorgeous blooms is rapturous. Rivaling the poinsettia for the title of seasonal icon, this bulb flower delivers the color and impact that the holiday demands. TIP: Avoid damage to delicate flowers like amaryllises by arranging them into the vase at bud stage and allowing them to open untouched. *Photo by John Collins*

LEFT Early in my flower arranging career, I was told that multiple colors of the same type of flower should never be mixed. Well, needless to say, that became something of a dare to me, as I have been looking to prove the notion wrong ever since. This wreath, composed of nothing but *Hypericum* berries, settles the score in my mind. TIP: Arrange each color of berries individually to create an evenly mixed mass.

Second only to color, texture is the design element that most captures the fancy of modern flower stylists. Quite simply, it makes the viewer want to reach out and touch. While a no-no in most art museums, for this composition of roses, berries, *Gloriosa* lilies, carnations and ming fern, it's absolutely allowed. TIP: This design was created on a jumbo designer block of floral foam. If an oversize block isn't available, multiple bricks can be hot-glued together before soaking in flower-food solution. *Photos by Stephen Smith*

Arranged in distinctive stripes, this pavéd tray of interesting textures brings an urban twist with its concrete container and manicured botanicals. TIP: Surround warm votives with mosses rather than fresh flowers, so the heat will not damage the blooms. *Photo by John Collins*

RIGHT While traditional styling dominates when it comes to holiday decorating, an occasional modern expression is refreshing and fun. This triptych of glass trays is filled with organic stripes of verdant *Hypericum* berries, deciduous holly (*Ilex*) branches, waxy lily grass and oxblood-colored fern fronds. TIP: Thread *Hypericum* berries onto a sturdy wire to hold them in place. *Photo by Stephen Smith*

credits

President of Florists' Review Enterprises: Frances Dudley, AAF
Publisher, Designer, Author: Talmage McLaurin, AIFD
Editor: Amy Bauer
Art Director: Linda Kunkle Park
Copy Editor: David Coake
Photographers: John Collins, Stephen Smith, Mark Robbins, Bill Boyd
Cover and Portrait Photos: Stephen Smith
Creative Coordinator: James Miller, AIFD

© 2011, Florists' Review Enterprises, Inc.

All Rights Reserved.
No part of this publication may
be reproduced without prior written
permission from the publisher.

Flower Styling was produced by Florists' Review Enterprises, Inc.,
Topeka, Kansas; www.floristsreview.com.

Printed in China.

ISBN: 978-0-9801815-7-9

Florists' Review Enterprises is the leading magazine and book publishing company for the U.S. floral industry. The company is home to *Florists' Review* and *Super Floral Retailing* magazines as well as to Florists' Review Bookstore, the industry's premier marketplace for books and other materials.

A special thanks to Transflora and Alexandra Farms
for providing flowers for the new photography in this book.